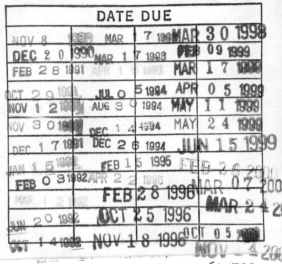

Fill It Up!
Copyright © 1985 by Gail Gibbons
Printed in the U.S.A. All rights reserved.
10 9 8 7 6 5 4 3

Library of Congress Cataloging in Publication Data
Gibbons, Gail.
  Fill it up!

  Summary: Describes a busy day at a gas station,
with cars coming in for gas or repairs.
  1. Automobiles—Service stations—Juvenile literature.
[1. Automobiles—Service stations.] I. Title.
TL153.G49 1985   629.28′6   84-45345
ISBN 0-690-04439-9
ISBN 0-690-04440-2 (lib. bdg.)

Special thanks to John Pierson of the Pierson Service Station,
Corinth, Vermont; John Sartory and Dennis Sullivan of the Shell Oil
Company; W. C. Stewart of the Exxon Company; Keith Welby of
Tri-Town Toyota, White River Junction, Vermont.

For Milton ("Joe the mechanic")

In the early morning the tow truck comes back from its first call of the day.

Out at the service islands customers are getting different kinds of gasoline.

Inside, in the office, bills are mailed out to customers.
New supplies are ordered.

The Service Station Day Crew

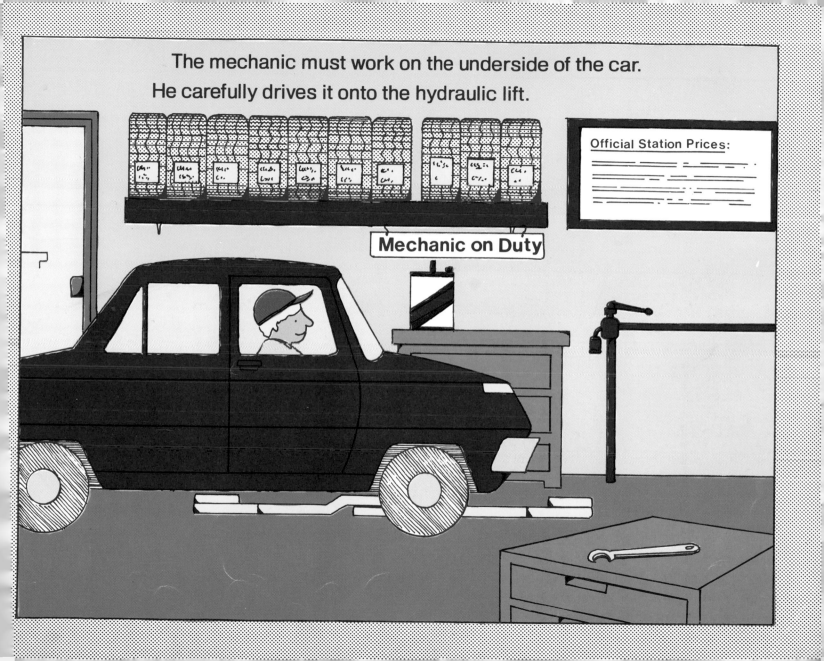

Here's how the hydraulic lift works.

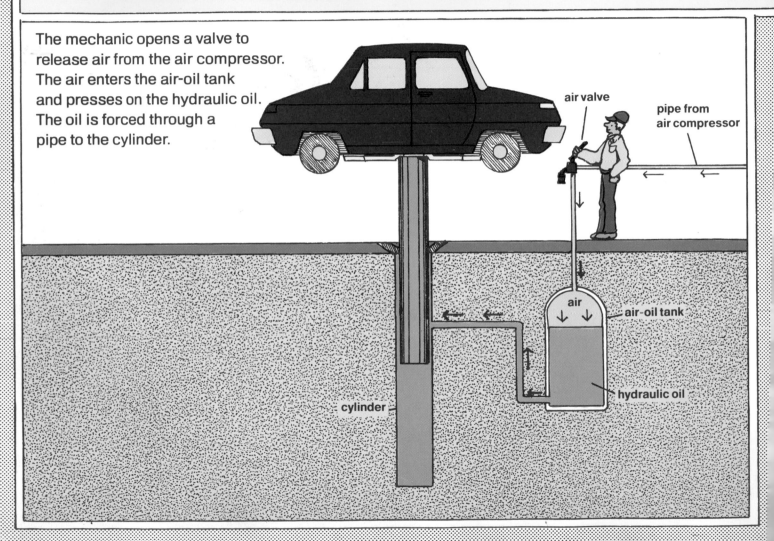

The mechanic opens a valve to release air from the air compressor. The air enters the air-oil tank and presses on the hydraulic oil. The oil is forced through a pipe to the cylinder.

air valve

pipe from air compressor

air

air-oil tank

hydraulic oil

cylinder

Inside the cylinder is a piston.
As more oil is forced into the cylinder,
the pressure makes the piston go up.
When the piston reaches the right height,
the mechanic shuts off the air valve
to stop the lift.

Now he can work under the car.

piston

Out front, a big truck pulls up to the diesel dispenser tank.

Another customer puts air into his tires.

Someone else wants directions.

For one driver, it's snack time.

The mechanic balances the tires so they will spin smoothly.

The new tires are put on the car. Then the mechanic checks the alignment of the wheels.

A truck comes with a new delivery of gasoline for the service station.

Here's where the gasoline is stored.

The gas is discharged from the truck into the separate underground storage tanks. These tanks hold the gas for the dispenser tanks at the service islands.

SELF SERVE

unleaded

super unleaded

regular

gasoline storage tanks

Here's how the gas is pumped.

Turning the lever on the side of the dispenser tank switches the pump on. Next, the hose nozzle is put into the opening of the car's gas tank. When the handle of the nozzle is pulled back, the pump pumps the gas.

The meter shows how much gas is going into the tank and how much it costs.

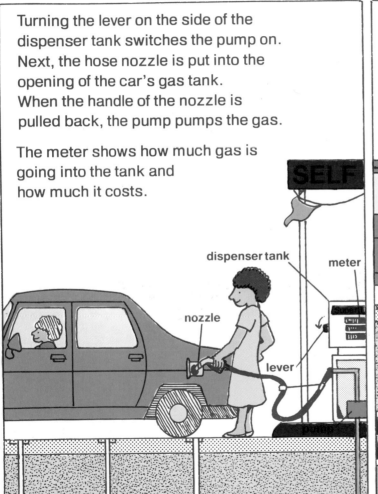

dispenser tank

meter

nozzle

lever

The gas moves from one of the big storage tanks through a pipe to the dispenser tank,

through the hose, out through the nozzle, and into the car's gas tank. When the right amount of gas is in the tank, the handle is released. The pump shuts off and the gas stops flowing. If the car's gas tank is filled to the top, the pump will automatically shut off.

Another car goes up on the hydraulic lift. The brakes need to be checked.

In the other bay a car is having its oil changed.

It's late afternoon. The cars and trucks have been coming and going all day long.

The pumps are always busy.

Here comes someone with a flat tire.

Here's how a flat tire is fixed.

The tire is filled with air. The sound of leaking air tells the mechanic where the cut is.

He uses a tire changer to pop the tire away from the rim.

The cut is patched.

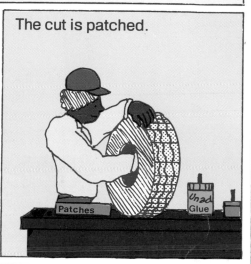

The tire is put back on the rim.

The tire is filled with air and balanced. Now it's ready to be used again.

Now it is evening. It is time for the day crew to go home.
There won't be any repair work done until tomorrow.
The evening crew arrives. They will keep the gas
dispensers pumping.

The customers come and go, and the evening crew works into the night.

After midnight only one attendant works at the station.
It is quiet. There are very few customers.

It's morning again. The day crew arrives. Today there will be more customers ... more cars to fix. ... And there goes the tow truck on the first call of the day.

Service Station Tools

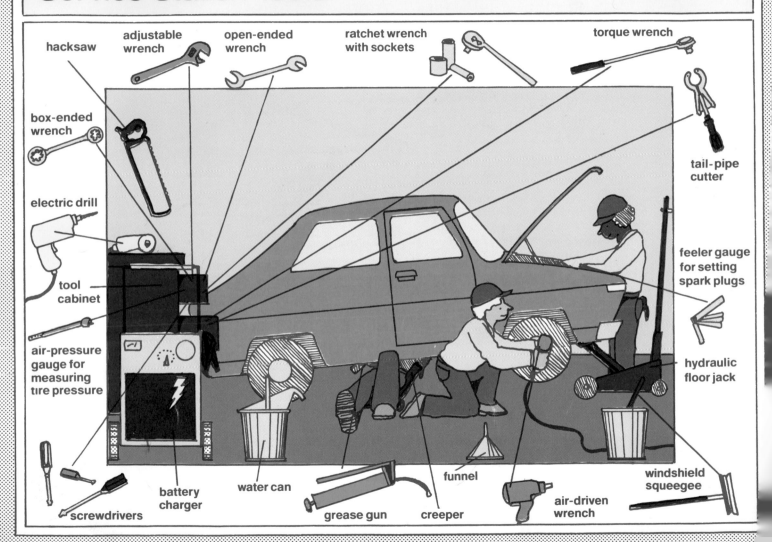

hacksaw

adjustable wrench

open-ended wrench

ratchet wrench with sockets

torque wrench

box-ended wrench

tail-pipe cutter

electric drill

feeler gauge for setting spark plugs

tool cabinet

air-pressure gauge for measuring tire pressure

hydraulic floor jack

screwdrivers

battery charger

water can

grease gun

creeper

funnel

air-driven wrench

windshield squeegee